The
BIBLE
PROMISE
BOOK
for
Couples

BARBOUR
PUBLISHING, INC.
Uhrichsville, Ohio

Published by Barbour Publishing, Inc.
        P.O. Box 719
        Uhrichsville, Ohio 44683
        http://www.barbourbooks.com

Member of the
Evangelical Christian
Publishers Association

Printed in the United States of America.

The

BIBLE
PROMISE
BOOK
for
Couples

TABLE OF CONTENTS

INTRODUCTION

Remember your wedding day? For many of us the memory may be a blur of flowers and lacy gowns, excitement and tension, tears and joy. The long anticipated day went by so quickly—and yet that was the beginning of our married life, the foundation of the years of love and patience and work that we've put into our marriage.

This book will give you a chance to relive that day, whether it was a year or two ago, or fifty years ago. As you walk in memory through the words of the marriage ceremony, let the words of Scripture sink into your hearts, enriching your marriage with the Holy Spirit's strength and love and joy.

Therefore, my brethren,
dearly beloved and longed for,
my joy and crown,
so stand fast in the Lord,
my dearly beloved.

Philippians 4:1

DEARLY BELOVED

. .we speak before God in Christ: but we do
ll things, dearly beloved, for your edifying.
2 Corinthians 12:19

/ly dearly beloved. . . Grace, mercy, and
eace, from God the Father and Christ Jesus
ur Lord.   *2 Timothy 1:2*

Jnto. . .our dearly beloved, and fellow la-
ourer,

Grace to you, and peace, from God our
ather and the Lord Jesus Christ.

I thank my God, making mention of
hee always in my prayers.

Philemon 1:1, 3–4

3ut we are bound to give thanks alway to
God for you, brethren beloved of the Lord,
ecause God hath from the beginning chosen you to salvation through sanctification
of the Spirit and belief of the truth.

2 Thessalonians 2:13

Therefore, brethren, stand fast, and hold
the traditions which ye have been taught,
whether by word, or our epistle.

2 Thessalonians 2:15

For where two or three
are gathered together
in my name,
there am I in
the midst of them.

Matthew 18:20

WE ARE GATHERED

When ye come together. . .let all things be done unto edifying.   *1 Corinthians 14:26*

. . .many were gathered together praying.
Acts 12:12

And when they were come, and had gathered the church together, they rehearsed all that God had done with them. . .   *Acts 14:27*

. .The Lord said unto me, . . . "Gather me the people together, and I will make them hear my words, that they may learn to fear me all the days that they shall live upon the earth, and that they may teach their children."   *Deuteronomy 4:10*

Gather the people together, men, and women, and children. . .that they may hear, and that they may learn, and fear the Lord your God, and observe to do all the words of this law.   *Deuteronomy 31:12*

Gather the people, sanctify the congregation, assemble the elders, gather the children. . . let the bridegroom go forth of his chamber, and the bride out of her closet.   *Joel 2:16*

Behold,
how good and how pleasant
it is for brethren to
dwell together in unity!

Psalm 133:1

TO UNITE

ndeavouring to keep the unity of the Spirit
the bond of peace.   *Ephesians 4:3*

ill we all come in the unity of the faith,
nd of the knowledge of the Son of God,
nto a perfect man, unto the measure of the
ature of the fulness of Christ.

Ephesians 4:13

nd they. . .did eat their meat with gladness
nd singleness of heart.   *Acts 2:46*

hat they all may be one; as thou, Father,
rt in me, and I in thee, that they also may
e one in us: that the world may believe
hat thou hast sent me.   *John 17:21*

here is neither Jew nor Greek, there is nei-
her bond nor free, there is neither male nor
emale: for ye are all one in Christ Jesus.

Galatians 3:28

Therefore shall a man leave
his father and his mother,
and shall cleave unto his wife:
and they shall be one flesh.

Genesis 2:24

IN MARRIAGE, ORDAINED OF GOD

And He answered and said unto them, Have ye not read, that He which made them at the beginning made them male and female?

And said, For this cause shall a man leave father and mother, and shall cleave to his wife: and they twain shall be one flesh?

Matthew 19:4–5

And the Lord God said, "It is not good that the man should be alone; I will make him an help meet for him."

And Adam said, "This is now bone of my bones, and flesh of my flesh: she shall be called Woman, because she was taken from Man."

Therefore shall a man leave his father and mother, and shall cleave unto his wife: and they shall be one flesh

Genesis 2:18, 23, 24

Nevertheless let every one of you in particular so love his wife even as himself; and the wife see that she reverence her husband.

Ephesians 5:33

Husbands, love your wives, even as Christ also loved the church, and gave himself for it.

Ephesians 5:25

Two are better than one. . .

For if they fall, the one will lift up his fellow. *Ecclesiastes 4:9–1*

Marriage is honourable in all. . .

Hebrews 13:

. . .Let every man have his own wife, and let every woman have her own husband.

Let the husband render unto the wife due benevolence: and likewise also the wife unto the husband.

The wife hath not power of her own body, but the husband: and likewise also the husband hath not power of his own body, but the wife. *1 Corinthians 7:2–4*

The kingdom of heaven is like unto a certain king, which made a marriage for his son,

. . .he sent forth other servants, saying, Tell them which are bidden, Behold, I have prepared my dinner: my oxen and my fatlings are killed, and all things are ready: come unto the marriage.

Matthew 22:2, 4

. . .Jesus was called, and his disciples, to the marriage. *John 2:2*

For thou, O God,
hast heard my vows.

Psalm 61:5

EXCHANGING SACRED VOWS

Offer unto God thanksgiving; and pay thy vows unto the most High.   *Psalm 50:14*

So will I sing praise unto thy name for ever, that I may daily perform my vows.
Psalm 61:8

If a man vow a vow unto the LORD, or swear an oath to bind his soul with a bond; he shall not break his word, he shall do according to all that proceedeth out of his mouth.

If a woman also vow a vow unto the LORD, and bind herself by a bond. . .

. . .then all her vows shall stand, and every bond wherewith she hath bound her soul shall stand.   *Numbers 30:2–4*

For then shalt thou have thy delight in the Almighty, and shalt lift up thy face unto God.

Thou shalt make thy prayer unto him, and he shall hear thee, and thou shalt pay thy vows.

Thou shalt also decree a thing, and it shall be established unto thee: and the light shall shine upon thy ways.   *Job 22:26–28*

. . .keep thy solemn feasts, perform thy vows. . .   *Nahum 1:15*

My praise shall be of thee in the great congregation: I will pay my vows before them
that fear him.   *Psalm 22:25*

. . .I will pay thee my vows,
   Which my lips have uttered. . .
                        Psalm 66:13–14

I will pay my vows unto the Lord now in
the presence of all his people.
                        Psalm 116:18

A new commandment
I give unto you,
That ye love one another;
as I have loved you,
that ye also love one another.

John 13:34

TO LOVE
AND TO CHERISH

Though I speak with the tongues of men and of angels, and have not charity [love], I am become as sounding brass, or a tinkling cymbal.

And though I have the gift of prophecy, and understand all mysteries, and all knowledge; and though I have all faith, so that I could remove mountains, and have not charity, I am nothing.

And though I bestow all my goods to feed the poor, and though I give my body to be burned, and have not charity, it profiteth me nothing

Charity suffereth long, and is kind; charity envieth not; charity vaunteth not itself, is not puffed up,

Doth not behave itself unseemly, seeketh not her own, is not easily provoked, thinketh no evil;

Rejoiceth not in iniquity, but rejoiceth in the truth;

Beareth all things, believeth all things, hopeth all things, endureth all things.

Charity never faileth: but whether there be prophecies, they shall fail; whether there be tongues, they shall cease; whether there be knowledge, it shall vanish away. . . .

And now abideth faith, hope, charity, these three; but the greatest of these is charity.   *1 Corinthians 13:1–8, 13*

There is no fear in love; but perfect love casteth out fear. . .

1 John 4:18

. . .see that ye love one another with a pure heart fervently.   *1 Peter 1:22*

For this is the message that ye heard from the beginning, that we should love one another.   *1 John 3:11*

And this is his commandment, That we should believe on the name of his Son Jesus Christ, and love one another, as he gave us commandment.   *1 John 3:23*

Beloved, let us love one another: for love is of God; and every one that loveth is born of God, and knoweth God. . . .

    Beloved, if God so loved us, we ought also to love one another.

    No man hath seen God at any time. If we love one another, God dwelleth in us, and his love is perfected in us.

1 John 4:7, 11–12

Husbands, love your wives, even as Christ also loved the church, and gave himself for it.   *Ephesians 5:25*

. . .teach the young women to be sober, to love their husbands, to love their children.

Titus 2:4

. .Intreat me not to leave thee, or to return from following after thee: for whither thou goest, I will go; and where thou lodgest, I will lodge: thy people shall be my people, and thy God my God:

Where thou diest, will I die, and there will I be buried: the LORD do so to me, and more also, if ought but death part thee and me. *Ruth 1:16–17*

Make a joyful noise
unto God, all ye lands:
Sing forth
the honour of his name:
make his praise glorious.

Psalm 66:1–2

FOR BETTER

Married life is full of many joys. The Scriptures speak of the many ways God blesses His children, with courage and encounters with His Spirit and faith; with forgiveness and growth and hope; with joy, patience, peace, and praise; with prayer, protection, sharing, thanksgiving, and wisdom.

COURAGE

Be strong and of a good courage, fear not, nor be afraid of them: for the LORD thy God, he it is that doth go with thee; he will not fail thee, nor forsake thee.

Deuteronomy 31:6

Have not I commanded thee? Be strong and of a good courage; be not afraid, neither be thou dismayed: for the LORD thy God is with thee whithersoever thou goest.

Joshua 1:9

Be of good courage, and let us behave ourselves valiantly. . .   *1 Chronicles 19:13*

. . .Deal courageously, and the LORD shall be with the good.   *2 Chronicles 19:11*

Arise. . .be of good courage, and do it.

Ezra 10:4

There shall not any man be able to stand
before thee all the days of thy life: as I was
with Moses, so I will be with thee: I will
not fail thee, nor forsake thee. *Joshua 1:5*

Wait on the LORD: be of good courage, and
he shall strengthen thine heart: wait, I say,
on the LORD. *Psalm 27:14*

Ye shall not need to fight in this battle: set
yourselves, stand ye still, and see the salvation of the LORD with you, O Judah and Jerusalem: fear not, nor be dismayed; to morrow
go out against them: for the LORD will be
with you. *2 Chronicles 20:17*

They helped every one his neighbour; and
every one said to his brother, Be of good
courage. *Isaiah 41:6*

But now thus saith the LORD that created
thee, O Jacob, and he that formed thee, O
Israel, "Fear not: for I have redeemed thee, I
have called thee by thy name; thou art mine.
    When thou passest through the waters,
I will be with thee; and through the rivers,
they shall not overflow thee: when thou
walkest through the fire, thou shalt not be
burned; neither shall the flame kindle upon
thee. . . .
    Since thou wast precious in my sight. . .
Fear not: for I am with thee. . ."
Isaiah 43:1–2, 4–5

Be ye therefore very courageous. . .that ye turn not aside therefrom to the right hand or to the left.   *Joshua 23:6*

Be of good courage, and he shall strengthen your heart, all ye that hope in the LORD.
                                        Psalm 31:24

Behold, I have made thy face strong against their faces. . .

. . .fear them not, neither be dismayed at their looks.   *Ezekiel 3:8–9*

Fear not, little flock; for it is your Father's good pleasure to give you the kingdom.
                                        Luke 12:32

Strengthen ye the weak hands, and confirm the feeble knees.

Say to them that are of a fearful heart, Be strong, fear not: behold, your God will come with vengeance, even God with a recompence; he will come and save you.
                                        Isaiah 35:3–4

Fear thou not; for I with thee: be not dismayed; for I am thy God: I will strengthen thee; yea, I will help thee; yea, I will uphold thee with the right hand of my righteousness. . . .

For I the LORD thy God will hold thy right hand, saying unto thee, Fear not; I will help thee.   *Isaiah 41:10, 13*

ENCOUNTERING GOD

. . .Lo, I am with you alway, even unto the end of the world. . . .   *Matthew 28:20*

. . .I have seen God face to face, and my life is preserved.   *Genesis 32:30*

But if from thence thou shalt seek the LORD thy God, thou shalt find him, if thou seek him with all thy heart and with all thy soul   *Deuteronomy 4:29*

I love them that love me; and those that seek me early shall find me.   *Proverbs 8:17*

And ye shall seek me, and find me, when ye shall search for me with all your heart.   *Jeremiah 29:13*

That they should seek the Lord, if haply they might feel after him, and find him, though he be not far from every one of us.   *Acts 17:27*

For now we see through a glass, darkly; but then face to face: now I know in part; but then shall I know even as also I am known.   *1 Corinthians 13:12*

FAITH

And Jesus said unto them. . . , "If ye have faith as a grain of mustard seed, ye shall say unto this mountain, Remove hence to yonder place; and it shall remove; and nothing shall be impossible unto you."   *Matthew 17:20*

For therein is the righteousness of God revealed from faith to faith: as it is written, The just shall live by faith.   *Romans 1:17*

Knowing that a man is not justified by the works of the law, but by the faith of Jesus Christ, even we have believed in Jesus Christ, that we might be justified by the faith of Christ, and not by the works of the law: for by the works of the law shall no flesh be justified.   *Galatians 2:16*

Above all, taking the shield of faith, wherewith ye shall be able to quench all the fiery darts of the wicked.   *Ephesians 6:16*

And the prayer of faith shall save the sick, and the Lord shall raise him up; and if he have committed sins, they shall be forgiven him.   *James 5:15*

FORGIVENESS

For if ye forgive men their trespasses, you heavenly Father will also forgive you.

But if ye forgive not men their tres passes, neither will your Father forgive you trespasses. *Matthew 6:14–1.*

Then came Peter to him, and said, "Lord how oft shall my brother sin against me, an I forgive him? till seven times?

Jesus saith unto him, I say not unto thee Until seven times: but, Until seventy time seven." *Matthew 18:21–2.*

And when ye stand praying, forgive, if ye have ought against any: that your Father also which is in heaven may forgive you you trespasses. *Mark 11:2.*

Judge not, and ye shall not be judged: con demn not, and ye shall not be condemned forgive, and ye shall be forgiven.

Luke 6:3

And forgive us our sins; for we also forgive every one that is indebted to us. . . .

Luke 11:4

If we confess our sins, he is faithful and just to forgive us our sins, and to cleanse us from all unrighteousness. *1 John 1:9*

Then said Jesus, "Father, forgive them; for they know not what they do. . . ."

Luke 23:34

In whom we have redemption through his blood, the forgiveness of sins, according to the riches of his grace. *Ephesians 1:7*

And be ye kind one to another, tenderhearted, forgiving one another, even as God for Christ's sake hath forgiven you.

Ephesians 4:32

And you, being dead in your sins. . .hath he quickened together with him, having forgiven you all trespasses;

Blotting out the handwriting of ordinances that was against us, which was contrary to us, and took it out of the way, nailing it to his cross. *Colossians 2:13–14*

In whom we have redemption through his blood, even the forgiveness of sins.

Colossians 1:14

Forbearing one another, and forgiving one another, if any man have a quarrel against any: even as Christ forgave you, so also do ye. *Colossians 3:13*

For thou, Lord, art good, and ready to forgive; and plenteous in mercy unto all them that call upon thee. *Psalm 86:5*

If thou, Lord, shouldest mark iniquities, O Lord, who shall stand?

But there is forgiveness with thee, that thou mayest be feared.   *Psalm 130:3–4*

. . .if he have committed sins, they shall be forgiven him.

Confess your faults one to another, and pray one for another, that ye may be healed.   *James 5:15–16*

To whom ye forgive any thing, I forgive also: for if I forgave any thing, to whom I forgave it, for your sakes forgave I it in the person of Christ.   *2 Corinthians 2:10*

If we confess our sins, he is faithful and just to forgive us our sins, and to cleanse us from all unrighteousness.   *1 John 1:9*

And when he saw their faith, he said unto him, "Man, thy sins are forgiven thee."   *Luke 5:20*

. . .Blessed are they whose iniquities are forgiven, and whose sins are covered.   *Romans 4:7*

Jesus. . .said, Son, be of good cheer; thy sins be forgiven thee.   *Matthew 9:2*

GROWTH

When I was a child, I spake as a child, I understood as a child, I thought as a child: but when I became a man, I put away childish things.   *1 Corinthians 13:11*

In whom all. . .together groweth unto an holy temple in the Lord.   *Ephesians 2:21*

. . .your faith groweth exceedingly, and the charity of every one of you all toward each other aboundeth.   *2 Thessalonians 1:3*

As newborn babes, desire the sincere milk of the word, that ye may grow thereby.
1 Peter 2:2

But grow in grace, and in the knowledge of our Lord and Saviour Jesus Christ.
2 Peter 3:18

That we henceforth be no more children. . .
But speaking the truth in love, may grow up into him in all things, which is the head, even Christ.   *Ephesians 4:14–15*

GUIDANCE FROM GOD

Lead me, O Lord, in thy righteousness because of mine enemies; make thy way straight before my face.   *Psalm 5:8*

O send out thy light and thy truth: let them lead me; let them bring me unto thy holy hill, and to thy tabernacles.

Psalm 43:3

But made his own people to go forth like sheep, and guided them in the wilderness like a flock.

And he led them on safely, so that they feared not: but the sea overwhelmed their enemies.

And he brought them to the border of his sanctuary. . .   *Psalm 78:52–54*

I lead in the way of righteousness, in the midst of the paths of judgment.

Proverbs 8:20

Trust in the LORD with all thine heart; and lean not unto thine own understanding.

In all thy ways acknowledge him, and he shall direct thy paths.   *Proverbs 3:5–6*

HOLINESS

Follow peace with all men, and holiness, without which no man shall see the Lord.

Hebrews 12:14

Thou art all fair, my love; there is no spot in thee.   *Song of Solomon 4:7*

. . .Ye shall be holy: for I the LORD your God am holy. *Leviticus 19:2*

As obedient children, not fashioning yourselves according to the former lusts in your ignorance:

But as he which hath called you is holy, so be ye holy in all manner of conversation. *1 Peter 1:14–15*

According as he hath chosen us in him before the foundation of the world, that we should be holy and without blame before him in love. *Ephesians 1:4*

HOPE

Therefore my heart is glad, and my glory rejoiceth: my flesh also shall rest in hope. *Psalm 16:9*

For in thee, O LORD, do I hope: thou wilt hear, O Lord my God. *Psalm 38:15*

And now, Lord, what wait I for? my hope is in thee. *Psalm 39:7*

Why art thou cast down, O my soul? and why art thou disquieted in me? hope thou in God: for I shall yet praise him for the help of his countenance. *Psalm 42:5*

For thou art my hope, O Lord GOD: thou art my trust from my youth. *Psalm 71:5*

Thou art my hiding place and my shield: I hope in thy word. *Psalm 119:114*

Uphold me according unto thy word, that I may live: and let me not be ashamed of my hope. *Psalm 119:116*

I wait for the LORD, my soul doth wait, and in his word do I hope. *Psalm 130:5*

The LORD is my portion, saith my soul; therefore will I hope in him. *Lamentations 3:24*

For whatsoever things were written aforetime were written for our learning, that we through patience and comfort of the scriptures might have hope. *Romans 15:4*

According to my earnest expectation and my hope, that in nothing I shall be ashamed, but that with all boldness, as always, so now also Christ shall be magnified in my body, whether it be by life, or by death.

Philippians 1:20

Now the God of hope fill you with all joy and peace in believing, that ye may abound in hope, through the power of the Holy Ghost. *Romans 15:13*

. . .God our Saviour, and Lord Jesus Christ, which is our hope. . . *1 Timothy 1:1*

The hope of the righteous shall be gladness: but the expectation of the wicked shall perish. *Proverbs 10:28*

Therefore did my heart rejoice, and my tongue was glad; moreover also my flesh shall rest in hope. *Acts 2:26*

Happy is he that hath the God of Jacob for his help, whose hope is in the LORD his God. *Psalm 146:5*

Hope deferred maketh the heart sick: but when the desire cometh, it is a tree of life. *Proverbs 13:12*

Blessed is the man that trusteth in the LORD, and whose hope the LORD is.

For he shall be as a tree planted by the waters, and that spreadeth out her roots by the river, and shall not see when heat cometh, but her leaf shall be green; and shall not be careful in the year of drought, neither shall cease from yielding fruit. *Jeremiah 17:7–8*

The wicked is driven away in his wickedness: but the righteous hath hope in his death. *Proverbs 14:32*

This I recall to my mind, therefore have I hope.

It is of the LORD'S mercies that we are not consumed, because his compassions fail not.

They arc new every morning: great is thy faithfulness.   *Lamentations 3:21–23*

But let us, who are of the day, be sober, putting on the breastplate of faith and love; and for an helmet, the hope of salvation.
    1 Thessalonians 5:8

The eyes of your understanding being enlightened; that ye may know what is the hope of his calling, and what the riches of the glory of his inheritance in the saints.
    Ephesians 1:18

. . .be not moved away from the hope of the gospel. . .

To whom God would make known what is the riches of the glory of this mystery among the Gentiles; which is Christ in you, the hope of glory.   *Colossians 1:23, 27*

There is one body, and one Spirit, even as ye are called in one hope of your calling.
    Ephesians 4:4

Looking for that blessed hope, and the glorious appearing of the great God and our Saviour Jesus Christ.   *Titus 2:13*

. .We glory in tribulations also: knowing that tribulation worketh patience;

And patience, experience; and experience, hope:

And hope maketh not ashamed; because the love of God is shed abroad in our hearts by the Holy Ghost which is given unto us.

Romans 5:3–5

JOY

. . .the joy of the LORD is your strength.

Nehemiah 8:10

. . .behold, I bring you good tidings of great joy, which shall be to all people.

Luke 2:10

. . .yet believing, ye rejoice with joy unspeakable and full of glory.   *1 Peter 1:8*

Be glad in the LORD, and rejoice, ye righteous: and shout for joy, all ye that are upright in heart.   *Psalm 32:11*

. . .God answereth him in the joy of his heart.   *Ecclesiastes 5:20*

For his anger endureth but a moment; in his favour is life: weeping may endure for a night, but joy cometh in the morning.

Psalm 30:5

But be ye glad and rejoice for ever in that which I create: for, behold, I create Jerusalem a rejoicing, and her people a joy.

And I will rejoice in Jerusalem, and joy in my people: and the voice of weeping shall be no more heard in her, nor the voice o crying.
Isaiah 65:18–19

And it shall be said in that day, Lo, this is our God; we have waited for him, and he will save us: this is the LORD; we have waited for him, we will be glad and rejoice in his salvation.
Isaiah 25:9

And the ransomed of the LORD shall return, and come to Zion with songs and everlasting joy upon their heads: they shall obtain joy and gladness, and sorrow and sighing shall flee away.
Isaiah 35:10

Although the fig tree shall not blossom, neither shall fruit be in the vines; the labour of the olive shall fail, and the fields shall yield no meat; the flock shall be cut off from the fold, and there shall be no herd in the stalls:

Yet I will rejoice in the LORD, I will joy in the God of my salvation.

The LORD God is my strength, and he will make my feet like hinds' feet, and he will make me to walk upon mine high places. . . .
Habakkuk 3:17–19

. . .we also joy in God through our Lord Jesus Christ, by whom we have now received the atonement. *Romans 5:11*

Thou hast turned for me my mourning into dancing: thou hast put off my sackcloth, and girded me with gladness. *Psalm 30:11*

LORD, lift thou up the light of thy countenance upon us.

Thou hast put gladness in my heart, more than in the time that their corn and their wine increased. *Psalm 4:6–7*

But let all those that put their trust in thee rejoice: let them ever shout for joy, because thou defendest them: let them also that love thy name be joyful in thee. *Psalm 5:11*

I will praise thee, O LORD, with my whole heart; I will shew forth all thy marvellous works.

I will be glad and rejoice in thee: I will sing praise to thy name, O thou most High. *Psalm 9:1–2*

Serve the LORD with gladness: come before his presence with singing. *Psalm 100:2*

This is the day which the LORD hath made; we will rejoice and be glad in it. *Psalm 118:24*

MERCY

Surely goodness and mercy shall follow me all the days of my life: and I will dwell in the house of the LORD for ever.   *Psalm 23:6*

All the paths of the LORD are mercy and truth unto such as keep his covenant and his testimonies.   *Psalm 25:10*

Many sorrows shall be to the wicked: but he that trusteth in the LORD, mercy shall compass him about.   *Psalm 32:10*

Withhold not thou thy tender mercies from me, O LORD: let thy lovingkindness and thy truth continually preserve me.

Psalm 40:11

He shall send from heaven, and save me from the reproach of him that would swallow me up. Selah. God shall send forth his mercy and his truth.   *Psalm 57:3*

But my faithfulness and my mercy shall be with him: and in my name shall his horn be exalted.   *Psalm 89:24*

Blessed be the God and Father of our Lord Jesus Christ, which according to his abundant mercy hath begotten us again unto a lively hope by the resurrection of Jesus Christ from the dead.   *1 Peter 1:3*

For the LORD is good; his mercy is everlasting; and his truth endureth to all generations.
Psalm 100:5

For thou, Lord, art good, and ready to forgive; and plenteous in mercy unto all them that call upon thee.

. . .a God full of compassion, and gracious, longsuffering, and plenteous in mercy and truth.
Psalm 86:5, 15

. . .I will have mercy on whom I will have mercy, and I will have compassion on whom I will have compassion.

So then it is not of him that willeth, nor of him that runneth, but of God that sheweth mercy.
Romans 9:15–16

Behold, we count them happy which endure. Ye have heard of the patience of Job, and have seen the end of the Lord; that the Lord is very pitiful, and of tender mercy.
James 5:11

Praise ye the LORD. O give thanks unto the LORD; for he is good: for his mercy endureth for ever.
Psalm 106:1

But God, who is rich in mercy, for his great love wherewith he loved us,

Even when we were dead in sins, hath quickened us together with Christ, (by grace ye are saved).
Ephesians 2:4–5

Let Israel hope in the LORD: for with the LORD there is mercy, and with him is plenteous redemption.   *Psalm 130:7*

O give thanks unto the LORD; for he is good: for his mercy endureth for ever.

O give thanks unto the God of gods: for his mercy endureth for ever.

O give thanks to the Lord of lords: for his mercy endureth for ever.

To him who alone doeth great wonders: for his mercy endureth for ever.

To him that by wisdom made the heavens: for his mercy endureth for ever.

To him that stretched out the earth above the waters: for his mercy endureth for ever.

To him that made great lights: for his mercy endureth for ever:

The sun to rule by day: for his mercy endureth for ever:

The moon and stars to rule by night: for his mercy endureth for ever. . . .

Who remembered us in our low estate: for his mercy endureth for ever:

And hath redeemed us from our enemies: for his mercy endureth for ever.

Who giveth food to all flesh: for his mercy endureth for ever.

O give thanks unto the God of heaven: for his mercy endureth for ever.

Psalm 136:1–9, 23–26

PATIENCE

But that on the good ground are they, which in an honest and good heart, having heard the word, keep it, and bring forth fruit with patience. *Luke 8:15*

In your patience possess ye your souls.
Luke 21:19

And not only so, but we glory in tribulations also: knowing that tribulation worketh patience. *Romans 5:3*

But if we hope for that we see not, then do we with patience wait for it.
Romans 8:25

For whatsoever things were written aforetime were written for our learning, that we through patience and comfort of the scriptures might have hope. *Romans 15:4*

Strengthened with all might, according to his glorious power, unto all patience and long-suffering with joyfulness.
Colossians 1:11

Remembering without ceasing your work of faith, and labour of love, and patience of hope in our Lord Jesus Christ, in the sight of God and our Father. *1 Thessalonians 1:3*

But thou, O man of God, flee these things;
and follow after righteousness, godliness,
faith, love, patience, meekness.

1 Timothy 6:11

That ye be not slothful, but followers of
them who through faith and patience inherit the promises.   *Hebrews 6:12*

For ye have need of patience, that, after ye
have done the will of God, ye might receive
the promise.   *Hebrews 10:36*

Wherefore seeing we also are compassed
about with so great a cloud of witnesses, let
us lay aside every weight, and the sin which
doth so easily beset us, and let us run with
patience the race that is set before us.

Hebrews 12:1

Knowing this, that the trying of your faith
worketh patience.   *James 1:3*

But let patience have her perfect work, that
ye may be perfect and entire, wanting nothing.   *James 1:4*

Here is the patience of the saints: here are
they that keep the commandments of God,
and the faith of Jesus.   *Revelation 14:12*

Rest in the LORD, and wait patiently for
him. . .   *Psalm 37:7*

I know thy works, and charity, and service, and faith, and thy patience, and thy works; and the last to be more than the first.

Revelation 2:19

I waited patiently for the LORD; and he inclined unto me, and heard my cry.

Psalm 40:1

PEACE

And I will give peace in the land, and ye shall lie down, and none shall make you afraid: and I will rid evil beasts out of the land, neither shall the sword go through your land. *Leviticus 26:6*

The LORD lift up his countenance upon thee, and give thee peace. *Numbers 6:26*

The LORD will give strength unto his people; the LORD will bless his people with peace. *Psalm 29:11*

Peace I leave with you, my peace I give unto you: not as the world giveth, give I unto you. Let not your heart be troubled, neither let it be afraid. *John 14:27*

To give light to them that sit in darkness and in the shadow of death, to guide our feet into the way of peace. *Luke 1:79*

Now the Lord of peace himself give you peace always by all means. The Lord be with you all. *2 Thessalonians 3:16*

And the peace of God, which passeth all understanding, shall keep your hearts and minds through Christ Jesus.

Philippians 4:7

Wherefore say, Behold, I give unto him my covenant of peace. *Numbers 25:12*

And let the peace of God rule in your hearts, to the which also ye are called in one body; and be ye thankful. *Colossians 3:15*

Depart from evil, and do good; seek peace, and pursue it. *Psalm 34:14*

But the meek shall inherit the earth; and shall delight themselves in the abundance of peace. . . .
    Mark the perfect man, and behold the upright: for the end of that man is peace.

Psalm 37:11, 37

I will hear what God the LORD will speak: for he will speak peace unto his people. . . .

Psalm 85:8

. . .I will cure them, and will reveal unto them the abundance of peace and truth.

Jeremiah 33:6

Happy is the man that findeth wisdom, and the man that getteth understanding. . . .

Her ways are ways of pleasantness, and all her paths are peace. *Proverbs 3:13, 17*

For unto us a child is born, unto us a son is given: and the government shall be upon his shoulder: and his name shall be called. . .The Prince of Peace.

Of the increase of his government and peace there shall be no end. . .

Isaiah 9:6–7

And the work of righteousness shall be peace; and the effect of righteousness quietness and assurance for ever.

And my people shall dwell in a peaceable habitation, and in sure dwellings, and in quiet resting places. *Isaiah 32:17–18*

For I know the thoughts that I think toward you, saith the LORD, thoughts of peace, and not of evil, to give you an expected end.

Jeremiah 29:11

These things I have spoken unto you, that in me ye might have peace. In the world ye shall have tribulation: but be of good cheer; I have overcome the world. *John 16:33*

. . .God hath called us to peace.

1 Corinthians 7:15

For he is our peace. . .   *Ephesians 2:14*

If it be possible, as much as lieth in you, live peaceably with all men.   *Romans 12:18*

Blessed are the peacemakers: for they shall be called the children of God.
Matthew 5:9

. . .Be perfect, be of good comfort, be of one mind, live in peace; and the God of love and peace shall be with you.
2 Corinthians 13:11

Thou wilt keep him in perfect peace, whose mind is stayed on thee: because he trusteth in thee.   *Isaiah 26:3*

But the wisdom that is from above is first pure, then peaceable, gentle, and easy to be intreated, full of mercy and good fruits, without partiality, and without hypocrisy.
And the fruit of righteousness is sown in peace of them that make peace.
James 3:17–18

PRAISE

In God we boast all the day long, and praise thy name for ever. Selah.   *Psalm 44:8*

In God will I praise his word: in the LORD will I praise his word.   *Psalm 56:10*

To the end that my glory may sing praise to thee, and not be silent. O LORD my God, I will give thanks unto thee for ever.

Psalm 30:12

And he hath put a new song in my mouth, even praise unto our God: many shall see it, and fear, and shall trust in the LORD.

Psalm 40:3

Why art thou cast down, O my soul? and why art thou disquieted within me? hope thou in God: for I shall yet praise him, who is the health of my countenance, and my God.

Psalm 42:11

Then will I go unto the altar of God, unto God my exceeding joy: yea, upon the harp will I praise thee, O God my God.

Psalm 43:4

Whoso offereth praise glorifieth me: and to him that ordereth his conversation aright will I shew the salvation of God.

Psalm 50:23

By him therefore let us offer the sacrifice of praise to God continually, that is, the fruit of our lips giving thanks to his name.

Hebrews 13:15

My heart is fixed, O God, my heart is fixed: I will sing and give praise.   *Psalm 57:7*

I will praise the name of God with a song, and will magnify him with thanksgiving.
Psalms 69:30

I will praise thee, O Lord my God, with all my heart: and I will glorify thy name for evermore. *Psalm 86:12*

I will sing unto the LORD as long as I live: I will sing praise to my God while I have my being. *Psalm 104:33*

Blessed be the Lord God of Israel from everlasting to everlasting: and let all the people say, Amen. Praise ye the LORD.
Psalm 106:48

Thou art my God, and I will praise thee: thou art my God, I will exalt thee.
Psalm 118:28

Praise ye the LORD: for it is good to sing praises unto our God; for it is pleasant; and praise is comely. *Psalm 147:1*

And a voice came out of the throne, saying, "Praise our God, all ye his servants, and ye that fear him, both small and great."
Revelation 19:5

Now therefore, our God, we thank thee, and praise thy glorious name.
1 Chronicles 29:13

Therefore with joy shall ye draw water out of the wells of salvation.

And in that day shall ye say, Praise the LORD, call upon his name, declare his doings among the people, make mention that his name is exalted. *Isaiah 12:3–4*

PRAYER

After this manner therefore pray ye: Our Father which art in heaven, Hallowed be thy name.

Thy kingdom come. Thy will be done in earth, as it is in heaven.

Give us this day our daily bread.

And forgive us our debts, as we forgive our debtors.

And lead us not into temptation, but deliver us from evil: For thine is the kingdom, and the power, and the glory, for ever. Amen.
Matthew 6:9–13

And all things, whatsoever ye shall ask in prayer, believing, ye shall receive.
Matthew 21:22

Rejoicing in hope; patient in tribulation; continuing instant in prayer. *Romans 12:12*

Hear my prayer, O LORD, and give ear unto my cry; hold not thy peace at my tears.
Psalm 39:12

Then hear thou from the heavens, even from thy dwelling place, their prayer and their supplications, and maintain their cause, and forgive thy people which have sinned against thee.   *2 Chronicles 6:39*

Let thine ear now be attentive, and thine eyes open, that thou mayest hear the prayer of thy servant, which I pray before thee now, day and night.   *Nehemiah 1:6*

My voice shalt thou hear in the morning, O LORD; in the morning will I direct my prayer unto thee, and will look up.
                    Psalm 5:3

But as for me, my prayer is unto thee, O LORD, in an acceptable time: O God, in the multitude of thy mercy hear me, in the truth of thy salvation.   *Psalm 69:13*

Continue in prayer, and watch in the same with thanksgiving.   *Colossians 4:2*

PROTECTION

Thou hast also given me the shield of thy salvation: and thy gentleness hath made me great.   *2 Samuel 22:36*

. . .Fear not. . .I am thy shield, and thy exceeding great reward.   *Genesis 15:1*

Fear thou not; for I am with thee: be not dismayed; for I am thy God: I will strengthen thee; yea, I will help thee; yea, I will uphold thee with the right hand of my righteousness.   *Isaiah 41:10*

Yea, though I walk through the valley of the shadow of death, I will fear no evil: for thou art with me; thy rod and thy staff they comfort me.   *Psalm 23:4*

For thou, LORD, wilt bless the righteous; with favour wilt thou compass him as with a shield.   *Psalm 5:12*

Happy art thou, O Israel: who is like unto thee, O people saved by the LORD, the shield of thy help, and who is the sword of thy excellency! . . .   *Deuteronomy 33:29*

But thou, O LORD, art a shield for me; my glory, and the lifter up of mine head.
                    Psalm 3:3

O Israel, trust thou in the LORD: he is their help and their shield. . . .

Ye that fear the LORD, trust in the LORD: he is their help and their shield.
                    Psalm 115:9, 11

Our soul waiteth for the LORD: he is our help and our shield.   *Psalm 33:20*

The LORD is my strength and my shield; my heart trusted in him, and I am helped: therefore my heart greatly rejoiceth; and with my song will I praise him.

The LORD is their strength, and he is the saving strength of his anointed.

Psalm 28:7–8

Above all, taking the shield of faith, wherewith ye shall be able to quench all the fiery darts of the wicked.   *Ephesians 6:16*

For the LORD God is a sun and shield. . .
Psalm 84:11

Every word of God is pure: he is a shield unto them that put their trust in him.

Proverbs 30:5

REST

There remaineth therefore a rest to the people of God.

For he that is entered into his rest, he also hath ceased from his own works, as God did from his.

Let us labour therefore to enter into that rest, lest any man fall after the same example of unbelief.   *Hebrews 4:9–11*

There the wicked cease from troubling; and there the weary be at rest.   *Job 3:17*

For ye are not as yet come to the rest and to the inheritance, which the LORD your God giveth you. *Deuteronomy 12:9*

Rest in the LORD, and wait patiently for him. . . *Psalm 37:7*

He maketh me to lie down in green pastures: he leadeth me beside the still waters.
    He restoreth my soul. . .
Psalm 23:2–3

. . .Come ye yourselves apart into a desert place, and rest a while. . . *Mark 6:31*

SHARING

He that despiseth his neighbour sinneth: but he that hath mercy on the poor, happy is he.
Proverbs 14:21

Every man according as he purposeth in his heart, so let him give; not grudgingly, or of necessity: for God loveth a cheerful giver.
2 Corinthians 9:7

. . .remember the words of the Lord Jesus, how he said, "It is more blessed to give than to receive." *Acts 20:35*

. . .freely ye have received, freely give.
Matthew 10:8

And if any man will sue thee at the law, and take away thy coat, let him have thy cloke also.

And whosoever shall compel thee to go a mile, go with him twain.

Give to him that asketh thee, and from him that would borrow of thee turn not thou away. *Matthew 5:40–42*

THANKSGIVING

Give thanks unto the LORD, call upon his name, make known his deeds among the people. *1 Chronicles 16:8*

O give thanks unto the LORD; for he is good; for his mercy endureth for ever.
1 Chronicles 16:34

It is a good thing to give thanks unto the LORD, and to sing praises unto thy name, O most High. *Psalm 92:1*

Enter into his gates with thanksgiving, and into his courts with praise: be thankful unto him, and bless his name. *Psalm 100:4*

Continue in prayer, and watch in the same with thanksgiving. *Colossians 4:2*

And let the peace of God rule in your hearts, to the which also ye are called in one body; and be ye thankful. *Colossians 3:15*

I will praise the name of God with a song,
and will magnify him with thanksgiving.

Psalm 69:30

Let us come before his presence with thanksgiving, and make a joyful noise unto him
with psalms. *Psalm 95:2*

For all things are for your sakes, that the
abundant grace might through the thanksgiving of many redound to the glory of God.

2 Corinthians 4:15

Being enriched in every thing to all bounti-
fulness, which causeth through us thanksgiving to God. *2 Corinthians 9:11*

Be careful for nothing; but in every thing by
prayer and supplication with thanksgiving
let your requests be made known unto God.

Philippians 4:6

For every creature of God is good, and
nothing to be refused, if it be received with
thanksgiving. *1 Timothy 4:4*

Giving thanks always for all things unto
God and the Father in the name of our Lord
Jesus Christ. *Ephesians 5:20*

Rooted and built up in him, and stablished in
the faith, as ye have been taught, abounding
therein with thanksgiving. *Colossians 2:7*

TRUTH

For thy mercy is great unto the heavens, and thy truth unto the clouds. *Psalm 57:10*

Now therefore fear the LORD, and serve him in sincerity and in truth. . .
Joshua 24:14

For the word of the LORD is right; and all his works are done in truth. *Psalm 33:4*

. . .The LORD liveth, in truth, in judgment, and in righteousness. . . *Jeremiah 4:2*

Teach me thy way, O LORD; I will walk in thy truth: unite my heart to fear thy name.
Psalm 86:11

God is a Spirit: and they that worship him must worship him in spirit and in truth.
John 4:24

Seeing ye have purified your souls in obeying the truth through the Spirit unto unfeigned love of the brethren, see that ye love one another with a pure heart fervently.
1 Peter 1:22

Charity. . .
Rejoiceth not in iniquity, but rejoiceth in the truth. *1 Corinthians 13:4, 6*

Lead me in thy truth, and teach me: for thou art the God of my salvation; on thee do I wait all the day. *Psalm 25:5*

Sanctify them through thy truth: thy word is truth. *John 17:17*

O send out thy light and thy truth: let them lead me; let them bring me unto thy holy hill, and to thy tabernacles. *Psalm 43:3*

Study to shew thyself approved unto God, a workman that needeth not to be ashamed, rightly dividing the word of truth.
2 Timothy 2:15

WISDOM

And I have filled him with the spirit of God, in wisdom, and in understanding, and in knowledge, and in all manner of workmanship. *Exodus 31:3*

With him is wisdom and strength, he hath counsel and understanding. *Job 12:13*

And unto man he said, Behold, the fear of the Lord, that is wisdom; and to depart from evil is understanding. *Job 28:28*

For the LORD giveth wisdom: out of his mouth cometh knowledge and understanding.
Proverbs 2:6

The fear of the LORD is the beginning of wisdom: a good understanding have all they that do his commandments: his praise endureth for ever.   *Psalm 111:10*

How much better is it to get wisdom than gold! and to get understanding rather to be chosen than silver!   *Proverbs 16:16*

And the spirit of the LORD shall rest upon him, the spirit of wisdom and understanding, the spirit of counsel and might, the spirit of knowledge and of the fear of the LORD.
Isaiah 11:2

Trust in the LORD with all thine heart; and lean not unto thine own understanding.
Proverbs 3:5

But the wisdom that is from above is first pure, then peaceable, gentle, and easy to be intreated, full of mercy and good fruits, without partiality, and without hypocrisy.
James 3:17

For wisdom is a defence, and money is a defence: but the excellency of knowledge is, that wisdom giveth life to them that have it.
Ecclesiastes 7:12

. . .be filled with the knowledge of his will in all wisdom and spiritual understanding.
Colossians 1:9

Wisdom is better than strength. . .

The words of wise men are heard in quiet more than the cry of him that ruleth among fools.

Wisdom is better than weapons of war. . . *Ecclesiastes 9:16–18*

Let no man deceive himself. If any man among you seemeth to be wise in this world, let him become a fool, that he may be wise.

For the wisdom of this world is foolishness with God. For it is written, He taketh the wise in their own craftiness.

1 Corinthians 3:18–19

Cast thy burden
upon the LORD,
and he shall sustain thee:
he shall never suffer
the righteous to be moved.

Psalm 55:22

FOR WORSE

During our married lives, sooner or later hard things come, like aging, anger, and discouragement; fear, misunderstandings, and pride; selfishness, temptation, and troubles. Through all of these, though, as we rely on God and His Scripture, we will find the strength to stay true to the marriage vows.

AGING

That thou mayest love the LORD thy God, and that thou mayest obey his voice, and that thou mayest cleave unto him: for he is thy life, and the length of thy days. . .
Deuteronomy 30:20

With the ancient is wisdom; and in length of days understanding. *Job 12:12*

He asked life of thee, and thou gavest it him, even length of days for ever and ever.
Psalm 21:4

For length of days, and long life, and peace, shall they add to thee. *Proverbs 3:2*

Length of days is in her right hand; and in her left hand riches and honour.
Proverbs 3:16

Cast me not off in the time of old age; forsake me not when my strength faileth. . .

Now also when I am old and greyheaded, O God, forsake me not; until I have shewed thy strength unto this generation, and thy power to every one that is to come.
Psalm 71:9, 18

With long life will I satisfy him, and shew him my salvation.   *Psalm 91:16*

For all our days are passed away in thy wrath: we spend our years as a tale that is told.

The days of our years are threescore years and ten; and if by reason of strength they be fourscore years, yet is their strength labour and sorrow; for it is soon cut off, and we fly away.   *Psalm 90:9–10*

Even to your old age I am he; and even to hoar hairs will I carry you: I have made, and I will bear; even I will carry, and will deliver you.   *Isaiah 46:4*

Thou shalt rise up before the hoary head, and honour the face of the old man. . .
Leviticus 19:32

Those that be planted in the house of the LORD shall flourish in the courts of our God.

They shall still bring forth fruit in old age; they shall be fat and flourishing.
Psalm 92:13–14

And if thou wilt walk in my ways, to keep my statutes and my commandments. . .then I will lengthen thy days.   *1 Kings 3:14*

The glory of young men is their strength: and the beauty of old men is the grey head.
                                    Proverbs 20:29

But continue thou in the things which thou hast learned and hast been assured of, knowing of whom thou hast learned them;

And that from a child thou hast known the holy scriptures, which are able to make thee wise unto salvation through faith which is in Christ Jesus.   *2 Timothy 3:14–15*

The hoary head is a crown of glory, if it be found in the way of righteousness.
                                    Proverbs 16:31

ANGER

Ye have heard that it was said by them of old time, Thou shalt not kill; and whosoever shall kill shall be in danger of the judgment:

But I say unto you, That whosoever is angry with his brother without a cause shall be in danger of the judgment: and whosoever shall say to his brother, Raca, shall be in danger of the council: but whosoever shall say, Thou fool, shall be in danger of hell fire.
                                    Matthew 5:21–22

Scornful men bring a city into a snare: but wise men turn away wrath. *Proverbs 29:8*

A soft answer turneth away wrath: but grievous words stir up anger. *Proverbs 15:1*

A wrathful man stirreth up strife: but he that is slow to anger appeaseth strife.
Proverbs 15:18

He that is slow to anger is better than the mighty; and he that ruleth his spirit than he that taketh a city. *Proverbs 16:32*

It is better to dwell in the wilderness, than with a contentious and an angry woman.
Proverbs 21:19

. . .Whosoever is angry with his brother without a cause shall be in danger of the judgment. . . *Matthew 5:22*

Let all bitterness, and wrath, and anger, and clamour, and evil speaking, be put away from you, with all malice. *Ephesians 4:31*

The north wind driveth away rain: so doth an angry countenance a backbiting tongue.
    It is better to dwell in the corner of the housetop, than with a brawling woman and in a wide house. *Proverbs 25:23–24*

Cease from anger, and forsake wrath: fret not thyself in any wise to do evil. *Psalm 37:8*

He that is soon angry dealeth foolishly. . .
Proverbs 14:17

Be ye angry, and sin not: let not the sun go down upon your wrath. *Ephesians 4:26*

A gift in secret pacifieth anger: and a reward in the bosom strong wrath. *Proverbs 21:14*

An angry man stirreth up strife, and a furious man aboundeth in transgression.
Proverbs 29:22

Be not hasty in thy spirit to be angry: for anger resteth in the bosom of fools.
Ecclesiastes 7:9

Wherefore, my beloved brethren, let every man be swift to hear, slow to speak, slow to wrath:

For the wrath of man worketh not the righteousness of God. *James 1:19–20*

For God hath not appointed us to wrath, but to obtain salvation by our Lord Jesus Christ.
1 Thessalonians 5:9

DISCOURAGEMENT

Behold, the LORD thy God hath set the land before thee: go up and possess it, as the LORD God of thy fathers hath said unto thee; fear not, neither be discouraged.

Deuteronomy 1:21

Though he fall, he shall not be utterly cast down: for the LORD upholdeth him with his hand. *Psalm 37:24*

I can do all things through Christ which strengtheneth me. *Philippians 4:13*

Why art thou cast down, O my soul? and why art thou disquieted in me? hope thou in God: for I shall yet praise him for the help of his countenance. *Psalm 42:5*

Nevertheless God, that comforteth those that are cast down, comforted us. . .

2 Corinthians 7:6

Rest in the LORD, and wait patiently for him: fret not thyself because of him who prospereth in his way, because of the man who bringeth wicked devices to pass.

Psalm 37:7

. . .we must through much tribulation enter into the kingdom of God. *Acts 14:22*

Hast thou not known? hast thou not heard, that the everlasting God, the LORD, the Creator of the ends of the earth, fainteth not, neither is weary? there is no searching of his understanding.

He giveth power to the faint; and to them that have no might he increaseth strength.

Even the youths shall faint and be weary, and the young men shall utterly fall:

But they that wait upon the LORD shall renew their strength; they shall mount up with wings as eagles; they shall run, and not be weary; and they shall walk, and not faint.

Isaiah 40:28–31

Although the fig tree shall not blossom, neither shall fruit be in the vines; the labour of the olive shall fail, and the fields shall yield no meat; the flock shall be cut off from the fold, and there shall be no herd in the stalls:

Yet I will rejoice in the LORD, I will joy in the God of my salvation.

Habakkuk 3:17–18

Blessed be God, even the Father of our Lord Jesus Christ, the Father of mercies, and the God of all comfort;

Who comforteth us in all our tribulation, that we may be able to comfort them which are in any trouble, by the comfort wherewith we ourselves are comforted of God.

2 Corinthians 1:3–4

And not only so, but we glory in tribulations also: knowing that tribulation worketh patience. *Romans 5:3*

. . .we faint not; but though our outward man perish, yet the inward man is renewed day by day.

For our light affliction, which is but for a moment, worketh for us a far more exceeding and eternal weight of glory.

2 Corinthians 4:16–17

FEAR

And, lo, the angel of the Lord came upon them, and the glory of the Lord shone round about them: and they were sore afraid.

And the angel said unto them, "Fear not: for, behold, I bring you good tidings of great joy, which shall be to all people."

Luke 2:9–10

Fear not, little flock; for it is your Father's good pleasure to give you the kingdom.

Luke 12:32

For God hath not given us the spirit of fear; but of power, and of love, and of a sound mind. *2 Timothy 1:7*

. . .Let not your heart be troubled, neither let it be afraid. *John 14:27*

And the LORD appeared unto him the same night, and said, "I am the God of Abraham thy father: fear not, for I am with thee, and will bless thee, and multiply thy seed for my servant Abraham's sake."   *Genesis 26:24*

Say to them that are of a fearful heart, Be strong, fear not: behold, your God will come with vengeance, even God with a recompence; he will come and save you.

Isaiah 35:4

And he saith unto them, "Why are ye fearful, O ye of little faith?" Then he arose, and rebuked the winds and the sea; and there was a great calm.   *Matthew 8:26*

. . .Dread not, neither be afraid of them.

The LORD your God which goeth before you, he shall fight for you. . .

Deuteronomy 1:29–30

I laid me down and slept; I awaked; for the LORD sustained me.

I will not be afraid of ten thousands of people, that have set themselves against me round about.   *Psalm 3:5–6*

. . .ye shall not be afraid of the face of man; for the judgment is God's: and the cause that is too hard for you, bring it unto me, and I will hear it.   *Deuteronomy 1:17*

He that dwelleth in the secret place of the most High shall abide under the shadow of the Almighty.

I will say of the LORD, He is my refuge and my fortress: my God; in him will I trust.

Surely he shall deliver thee from the snare of the fowler, and from the noisome pestilence.

He shall cover thee with his feathers, and under his wings shalt thou trust: his truth shall be thy shield and buckler.

Thou shalt not be afraid for the terror by night; nor for the arrow that flieth by day;

Nor for the pestilence that walketh in darkness; nor for the destruction that wasteth at noonday.

A thousand shall fall at thy side, and ten thousand at thy right hand; but it shall not come nigh thee. . . .

Because thou hast made the LORD, which is my refuge, even the most High, thy habitation;

There shall no evil befall thee, neither shall any plague come nigh thy dwelling.

For he shall give his angels charge over thee, to keep thee in all thy ways. . . .

Because he hath set his love upon me, therefore will I deliver him: I will set him on high, because he hath known my name.

He shall call upon me, and I will answer him: I will be with him in trouble; I will deliver him, and honour him.

Psalm 91:1–7, 9–11, 14–15

The fear of man bringeth a snare: but whoso putteth his trust in the LORD shall be safe.
Proverbs 29:25

In God have I put my trust: I will not be afraid what man can do unto me.
Psalm 56:11

In God I will praise his word, in God I have put my trust; I will not fear what flesh can do unto me.
Psalm 56:4

JUDGMENT

But with me it is a very small thing that I should be judged of you, or of man's judgment: yea, I judge not mine own self.

For I know nothing by myself; yet am I not hereby justified: but he that judgeth me is the Lord.

Therefore judge nothing before the time, until the Lord come, who both will bring to light the hidden things of darkness, and will make manifest the counsels of the hearts: and then shall every man have praise of God.
1 Corinthians 4:3–5

But why dost thou judge thy brother? or why dost thou set at nought thy brother? for we shall all stand before the judgment seat of Christ. . . .

So then every one of us shall give account of himself to God.

Let us not therefore judge one another any more: but judge this rather, that no man put a stumblingblock or an occasion to fall in his brother's way.

Romans 14:10, 12–13

MISUNDERSTANDINGS

Finally, be ye all of one mind, having compassion one of another, love as brethren, be pitiful, be courteous:

Not rendering evil for evil, or railing for railing: but contrariwise blessing. . .

1 Peter 3:8–9

Therefore if thou bring thy gift to the altar, and there rememberest that thy brother hath ought against thee;

Leave there thy gift before the altar, and go thy way; first be reconciled to thy brother, and then come and offer thy gift.

Matthew 5:23–24

Finally, brethren, farewell. Be perfect, be of good comfort, be of one mind, live in peace; and the God of love and peace shall be with you.　　*2 Corinthians 13:11*

. . .be likeminded, having the same love, being of one accord, of one mind.

Let nothing be done through strife or vainglory; but in lowliness of mind let each esteem other better than themselves. . . .

Let this mind be in you, which was also in Christ Jesus.   *Philippians 2:2–3, 5*

PRIDE

He hath shewed thee, O man, what is good; and what doth the LORD require of thee, but to do justly, and to love mercy, and to walk humbly with thy God?   *Micah 6:8*

Be not wise in thine own eyes: fear the LORD, and depart from evil.   *Proverbs 3:7*

When pride cometh, then cometh shame: but with the lowly is wisdom.   *Proverbs 11:2*

In the mouth of the foolish is a rod of pride: but the lips of the wise shall preserve them.
      Proverbs 14:3
Pride goeth before destruction, and an haughty spirit before a fall.
      Proverbs 16:18

For all that is in the world, the lust of the flesh, and the lust of the eyes, and the pride of life, is not of the Father, but is of the world.
      1 John 2:16

A man's pride shall bring him low: but honour shall uphold the humble in spirit.

Proverbs 29:23

Wherefore let him that thinketh he standeth take heed lest he fall.

1 Corinthians 10:12

SELFISHNESS

For I say, through the grace given unto me, to every man that is among you, not to think of himself more highly than he ought to think; but to think soberly, according as God hath dealt to every man the measure of faith.

Romans 12:3

Then Jesus beholding him loved him, and said unto him, "One thing thou lackest: go thy way, sell whatsoever thou hast, and give to the poor, and thou shalt have treasure in heaven: and come, take up the cross, and follow me."

And he was sad at that saying, and went away grieved: for he had great prossessions.

Mark 10:21–22

. . .charity envieth not; charity vaunteth not itself, is not puffed up,

Doth not behave itself unseemly, seeketh not her own, is not easily provoked. . .

1 Corinthians 13:4–5

And he spake a parable unto them, saying, "The ground of a certain rich man brought forth plentifully:

And he thought within himself, saying, What shall I do, because I have no room where to bestow my fruits?

And he said, This will I do: I will pull down my barns, and build greater; and there will I bestow all my fruits and my goods.

And I will say to my soul, Soul, thou hast much goods laid up for many years; take thine ease, eat, drink, and be merry.

But God said unto him, Thou fool, this night thy soul shall be required of thee: then whose shall those things be, which thou hast provided?

So is he that layeth up treasure for himself, and is not rich toward God."

Luke 12:16–21

SIN

For I know that in me (that is, in my flesh,) dwelleth no good thing: for to will is present with me; but how to perform that which is good I find not.

For the good that I would I do not: but the evil which I would not, that I do. . . .

O wretched man that I am! who shall deliver me from the body of this death?

I thank God through Jesus Christ our Lord. . . .   *Romans 7:18–19, 24–25*

But we are all as an unclean thing, and all our righteousnesses are as filthy rags; and we all do fade as a leaf; and our iniquities, like the wind, have taken us away. *Isaiah 64:6*

. . .Behold, I have caused thine iniquity to pass from thee, and I will clothe thee with change of raiment. *Zechariah 3:4*

Blessed is he whose transgression is forgiven, whose sin is covered. *Psalm 32:1*

. . .that I may win Christ,
And be found in him, not having mine own righteousness, which is of the law, but that which is through the faith of Christ, the righteousness which is of God by faith.
Philippians 3:8–9

TEMPTATION

There hath no temptation taken you but such as is common to man: but God is faithful, who will not suffer you to be tempted above that ye are able; but will with the temptation also make a way to escape, that ye may be able to bear it. *1 Corinthians 10:13*

Let no man say when he is tempted, I am tempted of God: for God cannot be tempted with evil, neither tempteth he any man.
James 1:13

Watch and pray, that ye enter not into temptation: the spirit indeed is willing, but the flesh is weak. *Matthew 26:41*

Abstain from all appearance of evil.
1 Thessalonians 5:22

Take ye heed, watch and pray: for ye know not when the time is. *Mark 13:33*

Harden not your heart, as in the provocation, and as in the day of temptation in the wilderness. *Psalm 95:8*

And lead us not into temptation, but deliver us from evil: For thine is the kingdom, and the power, and the glory, for ever. Amen.
Matthew 6:13

And when he was at the place, he said unto them, "Pray that ye enter not into temptation." *Luke 22:40*

And said unto them, "Why sleep ye? rise and pray, lest ye enter into temptation."
Luke 22:46

Because thou hast kept the word of my patience, I also will keep thee from the hour of temptation, which shall come upon all the world, to try them that dwell upon the earth.
Revelation 3:10

Blessed is the man that endureth temptation: for when he is tried, he shall receive the crown of life, which the Lord hath promised to them that love him.   *James 1:12*

TRAGEDY
AND TROUBLES

The spirit of the Lord GOD is upon me; because the LORD hath anointed me to preach good tidings unto the meek; he hath sent me to bind up the brokenhearted, to proclaim liberty to the captives, and the opening of the prison to them that are bound;

To proclaim the acceptable year of the LORD and the day of vengeance of our God; to comfort all that mourn;

To appoint unto them that mourn in Zion, to give unto them beauty for ashes, the oil of joy for mourning, the garment of praise for the spirit of heaviness; that they might be called trees of righteousness, the planting of the LORD, that he might be glorified.

Isaiah 61:1–3

How precious also are thy thoughts unto me, O God! how great is the sum of them!

If I should count them, they are more in number than the sand: when I awake, I am still with thee.   *Psalm 139:17–18*

Whither shall I go from thy spirit? or whither shall I flee from thy presence?

If I ascend up into heaven, thou art there: if I make my bed in hell, behold, thou art there.

If I take the wings of the morning, and dwell in the uttermost parts of the sea;

Even there shall thy hand lead me, and thy right hand shall hold me.

If I say, Surely the darkness shall cover me; even the night shall be light about me.

Yea, the darkness hideth not from thee; but the night shineth as the day: the darkness and the light are both alike to thee.

Psalm 139:7–12

Blessed are they that mourn: for they shall be comforted. *Matthew 5:4*

Blessed are they which are persecuted for righteousness' sake: for theirs is the kingdom of heaven. *Matthew 5:10*

Be not far from me; for trouble is near; for there is none to help. *Psalm 22:11*

God is our refuge and strength, a very present help in trouble. *Psalm 46:1*

Give us help from trouble: for vain is the help of man. *Psalm 60:11*

He that dwelleth in the secret place of the most High shall abide under the shadow of the Almighty.

I will say of the LORD, He is my refuge and my fortress: my God; in him will I trust.

Surely he shall deliver thee from the snare of the fowler, and from the noisome pestilence.

He shall cover thee with his feathers, and under his wings shalt thou trust: his truth shall be thy shield and buckler.

Thou shalt not be afraid for the terror by night; nor for the arrow that flieth by day.

Nor for the pestilence that walketh in darkness; nor for the destruction that wasteth at noonday.

A thousand shall fall at thy side, and ten thousand at thy right hand; but it shall not come nigh thee.

Only with thine eyes shalt thou behold and see the reward of the wicked.

Because thou hast made the LORD, which is my refuge, even the most High, thy habitation;

There shall no evil befall thee, neither shall any plague come nigh thy dwelling.

For he shall give his angels charge over thee, to keep thee in all thy ways.

They shall bear thee up in their hands, lest thou dash thy foot against a stone.

Thou shalt tread upon the lion and adder: the young lion and the dragon shalt thou trample under feet.

Because he hath set his love upon me, therefore will I deliver him: I will set him on high, because he hath known my name.

He shall call upon me, and I will answer him: I will be with him in trouble; I will deliver him, and honour him.

With long life will I satisfy him, and shew him my salvation.   *Psalm 91*

And he shall be
like a tree planted by
the rivers of water,
that bringeth forth
his fruit in his season;
his leaf also shall not wither;
and whatsoever he doeth
shall prosper.

Psalm 1:3

FOR RICHER

Through our married lives, God blesses us with all sorts of riches. Scripture speaks of the ways God prospers his children both spiritually and financially.

SPIRITUAL RICHES

That he would grant you, according to the riches of his glory, to be strengthened with might by his Spirit in the inner man.

Ephesians 3:16

. . .Except a man be born of water and of the Spirit, he cannot enter into the kingdom of God.   *John 3:5*

For the law of the Spirit of life in Christ Jesus hath made me free from the law of sin and death.   *Romans 8:2*

For they that are after the flesh do mind the things of the flesh; but they that are after the Spirit the things of the Spirit. *Romans 8:5*

But the natural man receiveth not the things of the Spirit of God: for they are foolishness unto him: neither can he know them, because they are spiritually discerned.

1 Corinthians 2:14

And he that searcheth the hearts knoweth what is the mind of the Spirit, because he maketh intercession for the saints according to the will of God. *Romans 8:27*

Who hath also sealed us, and given the earnest of the Spirit in our hearts.
2 Corinthians 1:22

Who also hath made us able ministers of the new testament; not of the letter, but of the spirit: for the letter killeth, but the spirit giveth life. *2 Corinthians 3:6*

Now he that hath wrought us for the selfsame thing is God, who also hath given unto us the earnest of the Spirit.
2 Corinthians 5:5

That the blessing of Abraham might come on the Gentiles through Jesus Christ; that we might receive the promise of the Spirit through faith. *Galatians 3:14*

How shall not the ministration of the spirit be rather glorious? *2 Corinthians 3:8*

But if ye be led of the Spirit, ye are not under the law. *Galatians 5:18*

If we live in the Spirit, let us also walk in the Spirit. *Galatians 5:25*

And take the helmet of salvation, and the sword of the Spirit, which is the word of God.
Ephesians 6:17

But the manifestation of the Spirit is given to every man to profit withal.
1 Corinthians 12:7

Endeavouring to keep the unity of the Spirit in the bond of peace.   *Ephesians 4:3*

For the fruit of the Spirit is in all goodness and righteousness and truth.
Ephesians 5:9

Lay not up for yourselves treasures upon earth, where moth and rust doth corrupt, and where thieves break through and steal:

But lay up for yourselves treasures in heaven, where neither moth nor rust doth corrupt, and where thieves do not break through nor steal"

For where your treasure is, there will your heart be also.   *Matthew 6:19–21*

FINANCIAL RICHES

And he shall be like a tree planted by the rivers of water, that bringeth forth his fruit in his season; his leaf also shall not wither; and whatsoever he doeth shall prosper.
Psalm 1:3

For every beast of the forest is mine, and the cattle upon a thousand hills. *Psalm 50:10*

Wealth gotten by vanity shall be diminished: but he that gathereth by labour shall increase. *Proverbs 13:11*

And I will multiply upon you man and beast; and they shall increase and bring fruit: and I will settle you after your old estates, and will do better unto you than at your beginnings: and ye shall know that I am the LORD.
Ezekiel 36:11

Only be thou strong and very courageous, that thou mayest observe to do according to all the law. . .turn not from it to the right hand or to the left, that thou mayest prosper whithersoever thou goest. *Joshua 1:7*

Then shalt thou prosper, if thou takest heed to fulfil the statutes and judgments which the LORD charged Moses with concerning Israel: be strong, and of good courage; dread not, nor be dismayed. *1 Chronicles 22:13*

. . .The God of heaven, he will prosper us; therefore we his servants will arise and build.
Nehemiah 2:20

. . .be content with such things as ye have: for he hath said, I will never leave thee, nor forsake thee. *Hebrews 13:5*

The LORD shall increase you more and more, you and your children.   *Psalm 115:14*

. . .The LORD gave Job twice as much as he had before.   *Job 42:10*

For thou hast been
a strength to the poor,
a strength to the needy
in his distress,
a refuge from the storm,
a shadow from the heat,
when the blast of
the terrible ones is as
a storm against the wall.

Isaiah 25:4

FOR POORER

Into all marriages come times when we have less. Whether we are lacking worldly wealth or spiritual, God can still bless our marriages in these times of need.

FINANCIALLY

I was a father to the poor. . . .   *Job 29:16*

He preserveth not the life of the wicked: but giveth right to the poor.   *Job 36:6*

. . .He hath dispersed, he hath given to the poor; his righteousness endureth for ever; his horn shall be exalted with honour.
Psalm 112:9

He hath dispersed abroad; he hath given to the poor: his righteousness remaineth for ever.   *2 Corinthians 9:9*

And I will feed. . .even you, O poor of the flock. . . .   *Zechariah 11:7*

IN SPIRIT

Better it is to be of an humble spirit with the lowly, than to divide the spoil with the proud.   *Proverbs 16:19*

For all those things hath mine hand made, and all those things have been, saith the LORD: but to this man will I look, even to him that is poor and of a contrite spirit, and trembleth at my word.   *Isaiah 66:2*

Blessed are the poor in spirit: for theirs is the kingdom of heaven.   *Matthew 5:3*

The LORD is nigh unto them that are of a broken heart; and saveth such as be of a contrite spirit.   *Psalm 34:18*

The sacrifices of God are a broken spirit: a broken and a contrite heart, O God, thou wilt not despise.   *Psalm 51:17*

For thus saith the high and lofty One that inhabiteth eternity, whose name is Holy; I dwell in the high and holy place, with him also that is of a contrite and humble spirit, to revive the spirit of the humble, and to revive the heart of the contrite ones.   *Isaiah 57:15*

. . .I am the LORD
that healeth thee.

Exodus 15:26

IN SICKNESS

Through the years, sickness strikes all marriages in some form or another. Body, mind, and soul, we need to lift ourselves and our partners up to God for His healing touch.

BODY

The LORD will strengthen him upon the bed of languishing: thou wilt make all his bed in his sickness.   *Psalm 41:3*

I shall not die, but live, and declare the works of the LORD.

The LORD hath chastened me sore: but he hath not given me over to death.

Psalm 118:17–18

Bless the LORD, O my soul, and forget not all his benefits:

. . .who healeth all thy diseases.

Psalm 103:2, 3

. . .My grace is sufficient for thee: for my strength is made perfect in weakness. Most gladly therefore will I rather glory in my infirmities, that the power of Christ may rest upon me.   *2 Corinthians 12:9*

MIND

That ye be not soon shaken in mind, or be troubled. . .as that the day of Christ is at hand. *2 Thessalonians 2:2*

I am forgotten as a dead man out of mind: I am like a broken vessel. *Psalm 31:12*

For God hath not given us the spirit of fear; but of power, and of love, and of a sound mind. *2 Timothy 1:7*

Thou wilt keep him in perfect peace, whose mind is stayed on thee: because he trusteth in thee. *Isaiah 26:3*

For ye have not received the spirit of bondage again to fear; but ye have received the Spirit of adoption, whereby we cry, Abba, Father. *Romans 8:15*

And the peace of God, which passeth all understanding, shall keep your hearts and minds through Christ Jesus.

Philippians 4:7

SPIRIT

Therefore I will not refrain my mouth; I will speak in the anguish of my spirit; I will complain in the bitterness of my soul.

Job 7:11

I remembered God, and was troubled: I complained, and my spirit was overwhelmed. . . .
Psalm 77:3

When my spirit was overwhelmed within me, then thou knewest my path. . . .
Psalm 142:3

Therefore is my spirit overwhelmed within me; my heart within me is desolate.
Psalm 143:4

Hear me speedily, O LORD: my spirit faileth: hide not thy face from me, lest I be like unto them that go down into the pit.
Psalm 143:7

O Lord, by these things men live, and in all these things is the life of my spirit: so wilt thou recover me, and make me to live.
Isaiah 38:16

And my spirit hath rejoiced in God my Saviour.
Luke 1:47

For I will restore
health unto thee,
and I will heal thee
of thy wounds,
saith the LORD.

Jeremiah 30:17

IN HEALTH

Health is a precious gift of God, a gift we can rejoice in when it comes to both us and our spouse, whether physically, mentally, or spiritually.

SOUNDNESS OF BODY

I will praise thee; for I am fearfully and wonderfully made: marvellous are thy works; and that my soul knoweth right well.

Psalm 139:14

. . .Daughter, be of good comfort: thy faith hath made thee whole; go in peace.

Luke 8:48

. . .Fear not: believe only, and she shall be made whole.   *Luke 8:50*

They that wait upon the LORD shall renew their strength; they shall mount up with wings as eagles; they shall run, and not be weary; and they shall walk, and not faint.

Isaiah 40:31

. . .thy youth is renewed like the eagle's.

Psalm 103:5

SOUNDNESS OF MIND

And be renewed in the spirit of your mind.
Ephesians 4:23

For God hath not given us the spirit of fear; but of power, and of love, and of a sound mind.
2 Timothy 1:7

And be not conformed to this world: but be ye transformed by the renewing of your mind, that ye may prove what is that good, and acceptable, and perfect, will of God.
Romans 12:2

Wherefore gird up the loins of your mind, be sober, and hope to the end for the grace that is to be brought unto you at the revelation of Jesus Christ.
1 Peter 1:13

SOUNDNESS OF SPIRIT

The Spirit itself beareth witness with our spirit, that we are the children of God.
Romans 8:16

But there is a spirit in man: and the inspiration of the Almighty giveth them understanding.
Job 32:8

Who hath also sealed us, and given the earnest of the Spirit in our hearts.
2 Corinthians 1:22

That he would grant you, according to the riches of his glory, to be strengthened with might by his Spirit in the inner man.

Ephesians 3:16

Can two walk together,
except they be agreed?

Amos 3:3

MUTUALLY AGREEING TO BE COMPANIONS

Behold, how good and how pleasant it is for brethren to dwell together in unity!
Psalm 133:1

Endeavouring to keep the unity of the Spirit in the bond of peace.   *Ephesians 4:3*

Again I say unto you, That if two of you shall agree on earth as touching any thing that they shall ask, it shall be done for them of my Father which is in heaven.   *Matthew 18:19*

Till we all come in the unity of the faith, and of the knowledge of the Son of God, unto a perfect man, unto the measure of the stature of the fulness of Christ.   *Ephesians 4:13*

For where two or three are gathered together in my name, there am I in the midst of them.
Matthew 18:20

A friend loveth at all times. . .
Proverbs 17:17

A man that hath friends must shew himself friendly: and there is a friend that sticketh closer than a brother.   *Proverbs 18:24*

And the LORD God said, "It is not good that the man should be alone; I will make him an help meet for him."

And out of the ground the LORD God formed every beast of the field, and every fowl of the air; and brought them unto Adam to see what he would call them: and whatsoever Adam called every living creature, that was the name thereof.

And Adam gave names to all cattle, and to the fowl of the air, and to every beast of the field; but for Adam there was not found an help meet for him.

And the LORD God caused a deep sleep to fall upon Adam, and he slept: and he took one of his ribs, and closed up the flesh instead thereof;

And the rib, which the LORD God had taken from man, made he a woman, and brought her unto the man.

And Adam said, "This is now bone of my bones, and flesh of my flesh. . ."

Genesis 2:18–23

Greater love hath no man than this, that a man lay down his life for his friends.

John 15:13

. . .For whither thou goest,
I will go;
and where thou lodgest,
I will lodge:
thy people shall be
my people,
and thy God my God.

Ruth 1:16

FORSAKING ALL OTHERS

Therefore shall a man leave his father and his mother, and shall cleave unto his wife: and they shall be one flesh.   *Genesis 2:24*

And Ruth said, "Intreat me not to leave thee, or to return from following after thee: for whither thou goest, I will go; and where thou lodgest, I will lodge: thy people shall be my people, and thy God my God."
Ruth 1:16

And said, "For this cause shall a man leave father and mother, and shall cleave to his wife: and they twain shall be one flesh?"
Matthew 19:5

Forsake her not, and she shall preserve thee: love her, and she shall keep thee.
Proverbs 4:6

Blessed are the pure in heart:
for they shall see God.

Matthew 5:8

KEEP YOURSELF HOLY

. . .neither be partaker of other men's sins: keep thyself pure.   *1 Timothy 5:22*

. . .teach the young women to be sober, to love their husbands, to love their children,

To be discreet, chaste, keepers at home, good, obedient to their own husbands, that the word of God be not blasphemed.
                                             Titus 2:4–5

A bishop then must be blameless, the husband of one wife, vigilant, sober, of good behaviour, given to hospitality, apt to teach.
                                             1 Timothy 3:2

Let the deacons be the husbands of one wife, ruling their children and their own houses well.   *1 Timothy 3:12*

Who shall ascend into the hill of the LORD? or who shall stand in his holy place?

He that hath clean hands, and a pure heart; who hath not lifted up his soul unto vanity, nor sworn deceitfully.
                                             Psalm 24:3–4

Holding the mystery of the faith in a pure conscience.   *1 Timothy 3:9*

Finally, brethren, whatsoever things are true, whatsoever things are honest, whatsoever things are just, whatsoever things are pure, whatsoever things are lovely, whatsoever things are of good report; if there be any virtue, and if there be any praise, think on these things. *Philippians 4:8*

Now the end of the commandment is charity out of a pure heart, and of a good conscience, and of faith unfeigned. *1 Timothy 1:5*

Flee also youthful lusts: but follow righteousness, faith, charity, peace, with them that call on the Lord out of a pure heart.
2 Timothy 2:22

Unto the pure all things are pure: but unto them that are defiled and unbelieving is nothing pure; but even their mind and conscience is defiled. *Titus 1:15*

Seeing ye have purified your souls in obeying the truth through the Spirit unto unfeigned love of the brethren, see that ye love one another with a pure heart fervently.
1 Peter 1:22

But the wisdom that is from above is first pure, then peaceable, gentle, and easy to be intreated, full of mercy and good fruits, without partiality, and without hypocrisy.
James 3:17

Let us draw near with a true heart in full assurance of faith, having our hearts sprinkled from an evil conscience, and our bodies washed with pure water.   *Hebrews 10:22*

And every man that hath this hope in him purifieth himself, even as he is pure.
                                        1 John 3:3

A faithful man
shall abound
with blessings. . .

Proverbs 28:20

KEEP YOURSELF
FOR EACH OTHER

Yet ye say, Wherefore? Because the LORD hath been witness between thee and the wife of thy youth, against whom thou hast dealt treacherously: yet is she thy companion, and the wife of thy covenant.   *Malachi 2:14*

There hath no temptation taken you but such as is common to man: but God is faithful, who will not suffer you to be tempted above that ye are able; but will with the temptation also make a way to escape, that ye may be able to bear it.   *1 Corinthians 10:13*

Even so must their wives be grave, not slanderers, sober, faithful in all things.
1 Timothy 3:11

Thou shalt not commit adultery.
Exodus 20:14

Thou shalt not covet thy neighbour's house, thou shalt not covet thy neighbour's wife, nor his manservant, nor his maidservant, nor his ox, nor his ass, nor any thing that is thy neighbour's.   *Exodus 20:17*

A virtuous woman is a crown to her husband: but she that maketh ashamed is as rottenness in his bones.   *Proverbs 12:4*

Who can find a virtuous woman? for her price is far above rubies.   *Proverbs 31:10*

Submit yourselves therefore to God. Resist the devil, and he will flee from you.
                                        James 4:7

Watch ye and pray, lest ye enter into temptation. The spirit truly is ready, but the flesh is weak.   *Mark 14:38*

Blessed is the man that endureth temptation: for when he is tried, he shall receive the crown of life, which the Lord hath promised to them that love him.   *James 1:12*

Let thy fountain be blessed:
and rejoice with
the wife of thy youth.

Proverbs 5:18

AS LONG AS YOU BOTH SHALL LIVE

Only take heed to thyself, and keep thy soul diligently, lest thou forget the things which thine eyes have seen, and lest they depart from thy heart all the days of thy life: but teach them thy sons, and thy sons' sons.

Deuteronomy 4:9

That thou mightest fear the LORD thy God, to keep all his statutes and his commandments, which I command thee, thou, and thy son, and thy son's son, all the days of thy life; and that thy days may be prolonged.

Deuteronomy 6:2

The LORD shall bless thee out of Zion: and thou shalt see the good of Jerusalem all the days of thy life. *Psalm 128:5*

So will I sing praise unto thy name for ever, that I may daily perform my vows.

Psalm 61:8

. . .Therefore take heed to your spirit, and let none deal treacherously against the wife of his youth. *Malachi 2:15*

**Wherefore
they are no more twain,
but one flesh. . . .**

Matthew 19:6

WHOM GOD HAS JOINED TOGETHER LET NO ONE PUT ASUNDER

And unto the married I command, yet not I, but the Lord, Let not the wife depart from her husband:

But and if she depart, let her remain unmarried, or be reconciled to her husband: and let not the husband put away his wife.

But to the rest speak I, not the Lord: If any brother hath a wife that believeth not, and she be pleased to dwell with him, let him not put her away.

And the woman which hath an husband that believeth not, and if he be pleased to dwell with her, let her not leave him.

For the unbelieving husband is sanctified by the wife, and the unbelieving wife is sanctified by the husband: else were your children unclean; but now are they holy.

But if the unbelieving depart, let him depart. A brother or a sister is not under bondage in such cases: but God hath called us to peace.

For what knowest thou, O wife, whether thou shalt save thy husband? or how knowest thou, O man, whether thou shalt save thy wife?   *1 Corinthians 7:10–16*

Wherefore they are no more twain, but one flesh. What therefore God hath joined together, let not man put asunder.

Matthew 19:6

The Pharisees also came unto him, tempting him, and saying unto him, "Is it lawful for a man to put away his wife for every cause?"

And he answered and said unto them, "Have ye not read, that he which made them at the beginning made them male and female,

And said, For this cause shall a man leave father and mother, and shall cleave to his wife: and they twain shall be one flesh?

Wherefore they are no more twain, but one flesh. What therefore God hath joined together, let not man put asunder."

They say unto him, "Why did Moses then command to give a writing of divorcement, and to put her away?"

He saith unto them, "Moses because of the hardness of your hearts suffered you to put away your wives: but from the beginning it was not so.

And I say unto you, Whosoever shall put away his wife, except it be for fornication, and shall marry another, committeth adultery: and whoso marrieth her which is put away doth commit adultery."

Matthew 19:3–9

What therefore God hath joined together, let not man put asunder. *Mark 10:9*

Then Joseph her husband, being a just man, and not willing to make her [Mary] a publick example, was minded to put her away privily.

But while he thought on these things, behold, the angel of the Lord appeared unto him in a dream, saying, "Joseph, thou son of David, fear not to take unto thee Mary thy wife: for that which is conceived in her is of the Holy Ghost."   *Matthew 1:19–20*

And her father hear her vow, and her bond wherewith she hath bound her soul, and her father shall hold his peace at her: then all her vows shall stand, and every bond wherewith she hath bound her soul shall stand.
                                            Numbers 30:4

Only thy holy things which thou hast, and thy vows, thou shalt take, and go unto the place which the LORD shall choose.
                                            Deuteronomy 12:26

It hath been said, Whosoever shall put away his wife, let him give her a writing of divorcement:

But I say unto you, That whosoever shall put away his wife, saving for the cause of fornication, causeth her to commit adultery: and whosoever shall marry her that is divorced committeth adultery.
                                            Matthew 5:31–32

The LORD bless thee,
and keep thee:
The LORD make his face
shine upon thee,
and be gracious unto thee:
The LORD lift up his
countenance upon thee,
and give thee peace.

Numbers 6:24–26

BENEDICTION AND BLESSING

Blessed are the poor in spirit: for theirs is the kingdom of heaven

Blessed are they that mourn: for they shall be comforted.

Blessed are the meek: for they shall inherit the earth.

Blessed are they which do hunger and thirst after righteousness: for they shall be filled.

Blessed are the merciful: for they shall obtain mercy.

Blessed are the pure in heart: for they shall see God.

Blessed are the peacemakers: for they shall be called the children of God.

Blessed are they which are persecuted for righteousness' sake: for theirs is the kingdom of heaven.

Blessed are ye, when men shall revile you, and persecute you, and shall say all manner of evil against you falsely, for my sake.

Rejoice, and be exceeding glad: for great is your reward in heaven: for so persecuted they the prophets which were before you.

Matthew 5:3–12

. . .Surely blessing I will bless thee, and multiplying I will multiply thee.

Hebrews 6:14

"And he blessed him, and said, Blessed be Abram of the most high God, possessor of heaven and earth." *Genesis 14:19*

The LORD shall bless thee out of Zion: and thou shalt see the good of Jerusalem all the days of thy life. *Psalm 128:5*

Grace be unto you, and peace, from God our Father, and from the Lord Jesus Christ.
1 Corinthians 1:3

Grace and peace be multiplied unto you through the knowledge of God, and of Jesus our Lord. *2 Peter 1:2*

Grace be with you, mercy, and peace, from God the Father, and from the Lord Jesus Christ, the Son of the Father, in truth and love. *2 John 1:3*

And all these blessings shall come on thee, and overtake thee, if thou shalt hearken unto the voice of the LORD thy God.
Deuteronomy 28:2

Blessed be the God and Father of our Lord Jesus Christ, who hath blessed us with all spiritual blessings in heavenly places in Christ. *Ephesians 1:3*

For length of days, and long life, and peace, shall they add to thee. *Proverbs 3:2*